Against Prompts

Against Prompts

Bill Yarrow

Lit
Fest
Press

Copyright © 2018 Bill Yarrow

ISBN: 978-1-943170-28-9

Cover Art Courtesy of Eryk Wenziak

Interior and Cover Design: Jane L. Carman

Published by Lit Fest Press, Carman, 688 Knox Road 900 North, Gilson, Illinois 61436

**Lit
Fest
Press**

Outside the box

for Leah

TABLE OF CONTENTS

Be Heuristic

Be Hubristic

Be Ekphrastic

Be Acoustic

Be Linguistic

Against Prompts

Be Heuristic

A THOUSAND BOOKS

I gave away 1000 books. Books I hunted.
Books I savored. Books I cared for.
Books I marked. Books I taught.
Books I browsed. Books I amassed.
Books others gave me. Books others
sold or abandoned. Books I kept.

I stuffed them in collection bins,
filled discard shelves, solicited readers,
advertised them, offered them,
boxed them, marked them,
hawked them, mailed them,
promised them, carried them,
scattered them, delivered them.

Once I thought I was made of books.

AUDEN AT SWARTHMORE

I was first in line that
Sunday, but it wasn't like
I hadn't heard other poets
read there. I had.

Rexroth, Berrigan, Padgett
Strand, Sidney Goldfarb
Jean Valentine, Daniel
Hoffman, Galway Kinnell.

They were known
or emerging but
not outlandishly famous
not like W. H. Auden.

So I went to see the wrinkled
and rumpled poet, who insisted
on reading from memory, stumbling
through his sheaf of poems.

Someone in the audience
should have heckled him
but everyone was in awe
of his assembled glory.

When I saw him, I was barely
twenty, and he was solidly
sixty four, years younger
than I am now.

Two years later, he died in Vienna.
That winter I returned to Philly
to see the exile Joseph Brodsky
read at the Broad Street Y.

He read his elegy to Auden, declaiming
Poetry without you equals only us.
"More blood! More adrenalin, you
parasite!" a young drunk cried.

Flailing his arms, yelling like
jealousy, the boy was dragged away.
Watching with grim interest, the future
Nobel Laureate bowed his dire head.

PAR DELICATESSE

I.

Rimbaud said, "Par delicatesse
j'ai perdu ma vie."
In the delicatessen,
I have lost my life.

I know what he meant.
I also have wandered among the smoked
fish, lean pastrami, marble rye, have
stood by the wicked pickle barrel, have
stared longingly at the crumbly halvah.

II.

Dante said one day he found himself
in a delicatessen ("selva oscura")
not knowing which aisle to walk down,
not knowing which meat to choose.
He too felt that he had lost his life.

I know what he meant.
I too have suffered paralysis
in a plethora of possibility:
belly or Nova, herring or tongue, chub or sable,
kreplach or kishke, kugel or blueberry blintz...

III.

Fitzgerald: "In the real dark night
of the soul, it is always three
o'clock in the delicatessen."
O lost! O lost! He lost his
compass in the schmaltz.

I know what he meant.
I've been in the 3 A.M. cream cheese.
I've known the hole in the bagel.
The potato knish is doughy. My life?
A shmere in a foreign appetite.

KNEECAPPING THE MUSE

In 1997, I was exploring a used bookstore in Camden, New Jersey, when I stumbled across a two-volume hardback copy of *The Dictionary of the Khazars* by Milorad Pavić, a book I had been meaning to read since it came out in 1984. At $10.00 for the set, I couldn't pass up the bargain, so I bought the books and rushed home with them. The volumes were quite handsome, orange dustjackets with bold red lettering, and quite pleasant to hold. I sat down in the wing chair in my bookroom and started to flip through them. Tucked midway in the second volume was one sheet of very thin paper covered, from top to bottom, from edge to edge, on both sides, with tiny, crimped handwriting. My curiosity was aroused. I tried to read what was written on the paper, but the writing was impossibly small. I couldn't decipher it with my naked eye. I got out a magnifying glass I had lying around but that didn't work, so I put the paper back in the volume and gave up.

Years later, I bought a printer that had a magnification function. I remembered the piece of paper in the book and played around with magnifying and printing as much of the paper as I could. After much experimentation and frustration, I was able to generate a fair amount of readable text but only from one side of the paper. The writing on the obverse side had deteriorated and could not be deciphered. I was, however, able to piece together those sections of text that, when magnified, often multiple times, were legible, so a portion of the document became clear. On the paper I discovered a narrative in labeled sections consisting of a "poem" of a mental patient followed by analyses of it by a doctor, a literary critic, and someone who claimed to be the patient's wife. The narrative ended, unfortunately, *in media res*. What follows is my best recreation of the substantial, but incomplete, part I was able, through much tedious effort, to recover.

I.

Poem of Patient A: "The Glittering"

> *Look, I couldn't help it. I took her. I took her*
> *dancing. In Strawberry Mansion. And the night*
> *expanded. And she was pressed up tight against*
> *me. And the music, though I was allergic, was*
> *magnetic. And I could feel her breasts all tense*
> *through her dress. But it was not like I was ever*
> *going to marry her, carry her across the merry*
> *threshold. She was not like the others, those*

archetypes, those mother types who had smothered
me with their tender needs, their needy tenderness.
Oh no. Oh no no no. That tactic did not attract me.
That resourcefulness did not ensorcell me. They were
not even appositely attractive. Just the opposite.
I was repelled. Impelled away. I rebelled. What did
I wish for when I was twenty two? Not just a woman.
A woman I could hold. Who would not hold me back.

I can still taste her perfume on my lips.

II.

The Doctor Will See You Now

An interesting case. Let's analyze the poem he wrote. Seems to me a poem about a man afraid to state the case. He can't admit his desire, the urge to "take" this woman, the free spirit, the anti-mother who doesn't want to get married as all the "others" do. He wants an unconventional girl—he's a rebel! Says "he took her" but only "took her dancing"! Then says the night "expanded." Interesting verb. But it wasn't the night that expanded; it was his pants, his penis, which she felt as "she was pressed up tight [*nota bene*] against" him. He wants to feel her breasts but he can write only that he could "feel" her breasts "all tense" and only "through her dress." Then there is the obsessive, almost pathological, triple wordplay—breasts-tense-dress, dancing-mansion-expan[sion], music-allergic-magnetic, marry-carry-merry, other-mother-smothered, tactic-attract-attractive, repelled-impelled-rebelled. One notices also the double wordplay (was he *incapable* of more triplets?): archetypes-mother-types, tender needs -needy tenderness, resourcefulness-ensorcell, appositely-opposite. Then unexpected alliteration kicks in in the last line—what-wish-when-was-woman—but one could argue it is echoed (or forecast) in the consonance of "K" sounds in line one. Finally, a concluding pun (holding the final ambiguity): "hold" vs. "not hold me back"—i.e. not return my embrace and not prevent me from fulfilling my desire. But the last line (separated) has none of the verbal yoga, none of the sonic contortions of the rest of the poem. A simple line. Iambic pentameter even. Well, pentameter but perhaps not iambic. The accents fall on "still," first syllable of "perfume," and on "lips." The return of the triple. Here three accents in a pentameter line. Lots of playing with threes and twos in the poem. Also a poem of seventeen lines, a prime number. His experience, he believes, is unique, indivisible. He craves the wildness of three but is reduced to the commonness of two. In the end, ordinary alliteration, dissolving into a paradox—something not to be resolved. Except by memory—something on his lips, but a scent not a kiss. A confusion of the senses. A confusion of intention. The poem of a man who thinks he knows exactly what he wants but who doesn't have a clue.

III.

The Literary Critic

I find the doctor's analysis interesting but wrong. His reading does not take into account the poem's title. Why is it called "The Glittering"? Doesn't the doctor find the title odd? There is, after all, no literal glittering in the poem itself. The title, clearly, is an allusion. We find the word in the following works:

1. Shakespeare's Henry IV, Part One:

   And like bright metal on a sullen ground,
   My reformation, glittering o'er my fault,
   Shall show more goodly and attract more eyes
   Than that which hath no foil to set it off.

2. Herrick's "Upon Julia's Clothes":

   Next, when I cast mine eyes, and see
   That brave vibration each way free,
   O how that glittering taketh me!

3. Boswell's Life of Johnson:

   He observed, that the established clergy in general did not preach plain enough; and that polished periods and glittering sentences flew over the heads of the common people, without any impression upon their hearts.

4. Dickinson 479:

   She dealt her pretty words like Blades—
   How glittering they shone—
   And every One unbared a Nerve
   Or wantoned with a Bone—

5. Whitman's "City of Ships"

   CITY of ships!
   (O the black ships! O the fierce ships!
   O the beautiful, sharp bow'd steam-ships and sail-ships!)
   City of the world! (for all races are here;
   All the lands of the earth make contributions here;)
   City of the sea! city of hurried and glittering tides!

6. Yeats's "Lapis Lazuli":

   Accomplished fingers begin to play.
   Their eyes mid many wrinkles, their eyes,
   Their ancient, glittering eyes, are gay.

7.   Auden's "Deftly, Admiral, Cast Your Fly":

> Salt are the deeps that cover
> The <u>glittering</u> fleets you led

Taken all together, the use of the word "glittering" suggests personal failure, sexual arousal, elaborate oratory, treacherous diction, animate Nature, wisdom, and warfare—all of which I find in the patient's poem. The author's personal failure is his sexual arousal (he "couldn't help it") expressed in euphuistic (i.e. over-elaborate or I might even say "treacherous") diction in which Woman's animate (smothering) nature mingles wily warfare ("tactic") and sweet wisdom ("perfume"). But what of *Strawberry* Mansion"? "Dancing" and "mansion" are half rhymes but why "strawberry"? What does a strawberry have to do with a mansion? Why is that particular fruit mentioned in the poem? Well, strawberry is, the doctor will surely attest to this, sexual slang and artists' icon for a woman's genitals. "Mansion" likewise, as in Yeats's "Crazy Jane Talks with the Bishop": "But Love has pitched his <u>mansion</u> in / The place of excrement." *Quod est demonstratum.*

IV.

<u>The Wife Has Her Say</u>

Strawberry Mansion. That's what intrigued me too. I wondered why it was capitalized

so I looked it up on Google. It's a section of Philadelphia where my husband's father was born. This leads me to wonder whether this poem is even about my husband. You both assume it is, but could it not also be about my father-in-law? None (or nearly none) of my husband's poems are about himself, even when he uses the "I." They are all persona (that's the right term, right?) poems, they all intuit (that's the verb my husband uses) a speaker, a speaker of some kind. I don't recognize my husband in the speaker in this poem. My husband is faithful. He's loving, he's kind. I married a veritable saint.

V.

<u>The Doctor Has a Question</u>

Why do you keep saying "my husband, my husband"? Why don't you refer to your husband by his name?

VI.

The Literary Critic Thinks He Knows

Why doesn't she call him by his name? Don't you see? She thinks her husband "saintly, faithful, loving, kind." There's no such husband! Never been such a husband! Who thinks like that? No one. A fictional character! I suspect this wife is pretend, a hired actress perhaps. I'm not even sure the patient is married. This may be just an act. I think he wrote those lines for her to say. There's a long respected tradition in literature for that kind of thing.

VII.

The Doctor Turns Suspicious

So you don't think a husband can be saintly, eh? That's interesting. What makes you say that? Why do you see that as an impossibility? What makes you so certain? Tell me about your own father. What was he like? How did he behave toward your mother? Was she

*   *   *   *   *   *   *

Here the manuscript breaks off.

PLAYING BOGGLE WITH LOWELL'S MIND

women   melon   news
omen   dwell   snow
mill   swim   mend
mold   swell   wild
wine   swill   mildew
lewd   sinew   swine
send   smell   doll
slow   sled   sell
smile   lemon   slime

In "Skunk Hour," Robert Lowell wrote, "My mind's not right." To see exactly what was in Lowell's mind, I wrote this poem made entirely of anagrams of four or more letters from the phrase "Lowell's mind."

Against Prompts

END GAME

Where the Story Lies

Everybody wants to know
where the story lies. Does it
lie in childhood? Does it lie
in old age? Does it lie in an
angry outburst or a stinging
rebuke? Does it lie in a moment
of compassion or in the recognition
of calloused selfishness? Bruised
love or hidden despair? Unfounded
ego? Personally, I couldn't care less
where the story lies. I care only
where the story tells the truth.

Where the Story Tells the Truth

Can a story tell the truth? What truth?
The truth of a moment? What good is that?
A good story is an honest story, but
honesty is not the same as truth.
Anderson's "Untold Lie" is a good story.
In that story, Hal Winters, twenty-two,
asks Ray Pearson, just fifty with six kids,
whether he should marry his pregnant
girlfriend Nell. Ray mulls it over, finally
deciding to tell him "No! Don't do it!" but
before he can say anything, Hal tells him
he's decided to marry her. Ray thinks, "It's
just as well. Whatever I told him would have
been a lie." See what I mean? Honest, yes,
but that's not at all the same as the truth.

Why Stories Can't Tell the Truth

Look, even a great story like Delmore Schwartz's
"In Dreams Begin Responsibilities," which tries
to tell the truth, can't help but fail. Remember
the story? A kid in a movie theater sees on the

screen his parents in their courting days. Like
Lambert Strether in *The Ambassadors,* he tries
to warn them: "Don't do it! It's not too late
to change your minds!" He gets thrown out
by the usher. He's about to turn twenty one.
That's where the story ends. That's the problem.
That's the essence of the problem. It's the problem
with every story, every novel, every play, every poem.
Stories end. Novels end. Plays end. Poems end.
The truth doesn't end. It doesn't pretend to.

Every Ending Is False

Every ending is false as every beginning is false
because every ending is arbitrary as every
beginning is arbitrary. We pretend otherwise,
but our life does not commence with our birth
(had we no parents or ancestors?) nor end with
our death (had we no influence or effect?)
We didn't begin; neither do we end. Just because
a book by us or about us has a first and last page
doesn't mean that we do also. We've never not
been here (we were potential in everyone who
came before us) and we'll never not be here (we
persist in some way in everyone who succeeds us)
and therefore every ending is false. This one too.

Not Every Ending Is False
for Marshall Levin

Though arbitrary, not every ending is false.
Better to say not every ending is accurate.
To the extent to which no story reaches
a final conclusion, the most we can do
is echo Dostoyevsky:

> That might be the subject
> of a new story

        but our present story
        is ended

We are the past story, the present story,
and also the new story, the future story.
We end as a stanza ends, as a chapter ends.
Our book is not just long—it is endless.

Blake said

        One thought fills immensity

I say, one person fills eternity.

THE BODY IN THE OTHER ROOM

I couldn't parse the grammar of her body
nor decode the secret softness of her neck.
I didn't learn the tango of her shining
nor even once track the trespass of her tongue.
No one could rob her being of its bullion
or untie the satin lashes of her charm.
I lay with her on a tarnished beach at noon.
Above us, blind seagulls interrogated
aqueous clouds. I whispered a sinuous ...

I could go on but I'm tired, tired of
describing what doesn't exist, what never
existed, except in words, words, whorish words
of a certain alignment, a certain
innocuous provocative vicinity.

SELF INVENTORY

Sleep like a bear grabs you and won't let go.
Hunger is an ever-opening wound,
brashness a rash whose sudden appearance
is mysterious and unnerving like
a long film dissolve. Dreams, too, linger in
wild, new schemes. Your intelligence feels like
a weapon that's been fired in battle
but never been cleaned. Now regret, like a
bus backfire at 3 AM, has startled
you out of your chair. Generosity,
like a foreign city you always meant
to visit, stares at you with pleading eyes.
You're ashamed of selfishness, that blanket
whose softness and warmth you cannot give up.
Tolerance: dollars in someone else's
wallet. Arrogance: cake in the mouth of
a man too old to still be eating cake.
Life, like a kite string, is slipping out of
your hands. Wait: is *any* of this true? No.
Poems are not made of nothing but the truth.

Be Hubristic

ARCADE

My father owned a penny arcade. I worked for him every summer all during my youth. My job was to hand green tickets to customers who achieved a certain score on Skee-Ball or shuffleboard. The coupons could be redeemed for merchandise which we had on display on shelves on the walls and in showcases surrounding the cash register.

It was a boring job, walking up and down the rows of games, handing out coupons to kids and adults, trying to be there when they finished their game, explaining when I had to what the coupons were for, how many you needed to get something, etc.

Every day was the same, except for the times when the buses came in.

The buses brought in the groups.

A group of hearing-impaired students from a nearby college. Their hands were flags, like the semaphore flags of the lifeguards on the beach. They signed their excitement to each other.

A group from a mental institution. Microcephalics mostly. Some kids with Down syndrome. Other conditions. But happy.

And then there were the Thalidomide babies, all grown up, handsome boys and beautiful girls, playing Skee-Ball with flipper arms, throwing balls up the lane toward their numbered targets with their feet. I gave them their coupons as I did all the others but inside I shuddered. It was 1963. I was twelve.

I didn't understand what I was looking at.

My dreams did.

For the next twenty years, I had recurring nightmares about Thalidomide babies playing Skee-Ball, their stunted arms and feet becoming more and more marine, blending with images of puffer fish and shark fins and shiny black mussels and horseshoe crabs.

Wikipedia:

The drug, developed by Heinrich Mückter, began distribution in 1957. Used to treat symptoms of morning sickness. Withdrawn from the market in 1961 for causing birth defects. About 20,000 babies worldwide developed phocomelia. Was later used in the treatment of leprosy. Used today in the treatment of cancer.

Drugs never die.

The heinous becomes the useful.

In our arcade, the arcade that was torn down in 1978, twenty grown-up Thalidomide babies are still playing Skee-Ball.

> "Why are their arms like that?" I ask my mother.
> "Their mothers took a drug that caused birth defects," she tells me.
>
> "Why are they bowling with their feet?" I ask my father.
> "It's the only way they can play," he tells me.
>
> "What would you like for your coupons?" I ask them.
> "What can I get for this many?" they ask me.

WHOAMI

I am running around the perimeter of a collective farm at dawn. In the distance is a mountain made pink by a faint sun shining wanly on its highest snow. Four guards in four watchtowers search the surrounding terrain for attempted terrorists. This is my daily exercise, which I hope to complete before I engage in my daily chores: milking the cows, feeding the chickens, scrubbing the dining hall, policing the yard for trash. I see the sculptor emerge from his hut with his tools. A woman with fallen breasts is attempting to hang her laundry on a string. Two tall men mount horses and ride them into the meadow. A squad of children wrap themselves around a playground. The sentence of Proust I memorized last night before going to bed has fled my memory. I remember only the first word: "I." One of the elders signals to me to stop running; I am needed in the dining hall. A part of the ceiling near the pantry has come down. It will take six of us to push it firmly back into place. As I walk toward my task, I smell the heliotrope on the pubescent necks of the adolescent nannies assembled like Biblical wives circling the community well.

TRIPE AND COCAINE

A guy I knew on kibbutz
invited me to visit him
in Sheffield if I ever got
to England, so... I did.
"Come for dinner," he said.

It was raining or maybe
it wasn't as I climbed four
flights of dirty stairs and sat
on his filthy floor politely
declining a bowl of floating
tripe and a pencil line of coke.

I was not yet familiar with
the photos of Nan Goldin
but as I sat in Andy's flat,
I was also smack in that
depressing world, my fear
part of my excitement,
my repulsion the essence
of an untoward attraction.

I don't remember how long
I stayed or what else I didn't
do. It was raining I remember
as I wobbled back to my hotel
room hours after midnight.

Why this memory
after *all* this time
as I was driving
driving on I-55?

Why *this* memory
after all *this* time
as I was driving
driving on I-55?

Why this *memory*
after all this *time*
as I was driving
driving on I-55?

I am pursued   /   \   born in the   /   \   keep punching

pursued || || *in the* || || *punching*

by memories   \   /   head which   \   /   at the gut

SPEAKING TO THE DEAD

I didn't hear your last words or see your last
eyes. I didn't reach you in time, so I sat by your corpse,
silently saying goodbye. I am in that process,

not sour, not sweet, that yoked speaking which can't
(because the heart won't let it) utter its whispered
last word, but stutters instead like the awful-eyed

idiot of love, stroking a hand and thinking it speech.
Nothing pulses now from your cold, dead palm;
No sounds exit, no language leaks.

You're beyond the infinite weakness of words;
I'm still in their thrall, caught in the thrashing
eloquence of unregistered inarticulate emotion.

What does death do? It petrifies pain, reifies
loss, installs nothing new, revokes everything old.

COUPLEHOOD: YEAR SEVEN

She feels like an overheated car making a left turn into a fire pit.
He feels like a Mexican intestine.

She feels like a meatloaf donut.
He feels like a metadata omelet.

She feels like an aneurysm in someone else's cancer.
He feels like the impossibility of stumbling upon two emeralds seven miles apart.

She feels like the torn tendon of mistaken ambition.
He feels like a feline supine Christ.

UNSEENLY

Over the years, his face
began to alter, becoming
not round but rounder

not kind but kinder, not
ruddy but red, the map
of his complexion now

filled in with rivers of
creases, lakes of dis-
coloration, saharas of

psoriasis, waterfalls
of burst veins, tufts
of vegetation sprout-

ing with no or ungainly
purpose from above his
eyes or within his ears

not to mention the adjacent
crow's feet, perpendicular
laugh lines, frown lines

and evidence of a habitual
bit lip, all these things
and others, about which

acquaintances commented
with savage nonchalance
"It's not age, but character"

but to him it seemed rather
as if all his secret sins had
become suddenly visible.

GET A GRIP

There's a hole in my brain
out of which pour all my
good impulses and so I sit
at the Table of Behavior

next to the Witch of Logic
who kicks me whenever
Lady Compassion bats her
eyes at me, so heed this:

whosoever talks with me
talks not with me but with
that part of me that I resent
with all that's left of my heart.

EVERY SO OFTEN

Every so often I do something
Every so often I remember something
Every so often I write something

Every so often I think something
Every so often I feel something
Every so often I write something

Every so often I say something
Every so often I touch something
Every so often I write something

Every so often I neglect to do something
Every so often I forget to say something
Every so often I refuse to write something

Be Ekphrastic

DALI'S TEMPTATION OF ST. ANTHONY

teMp tation

always

comes   to/us

as hairy algebrA

in   our   rancid

nakednes-s

wE   can   offeR:back

only the fractured

icons of raDiant

ge

om

e

tr

yyyYyyy

JOHN OF GOD, PAINTED BY MURILLO

pictures a kneeling man in a monk's robe
lifting a naked beggar onto his shoulder

a bright light coming from the upper left
corner of the canvas attracts his attention

turning, he sees a winged dark-haired boy
in a gold dress stretch out his arm in aid

NO ONE CAN BE A BASTARD FOREVER!

WAYS OF SEEING: CARRACCI

I have become interested in Carracci—
Ludovico Carracci, Bolognese
contemporary of Shakespeare
early Baroque artist, cousin
of Agostino and Annibale

whose 1612 painting
Body of Saint Sebastian
Thrown into the Cloaca Maxima
is a masterpiece
of the frozen moment

Sebastian is limp in a sheet supported by
muscular soldiers. His hands hang down,
his eyes are shut. Is he asleep? More likely
unconscious. After all, he is about to be
thrown into the great sewer of Rome

Unless one rotates the image:
then he becomes beautifully
vertical, his dreaming body
like a sleeping bird floating
in warm, soft air

Then the closed fists and flexed
forearms of the executioners
are seen impotently attempting
to hold him down but nothing
human can prevent his rise

LEGAL IS THE TENDER
("Der arme Poet" by Carl Spitzweg)

Ay, pobre! Cold and counting out
your rhymes. You with the feather
in your mouth and your umbrella
nailed to the ceiling of your room.
Wake up and smell the sestinas.
Your servant Antiquo is on the way in
to bring you the nutmeg coffee and
angel cake of inspiration.

                              Stop!
That's enough. Why are you
describing a painting? To what
end? You have nothing of your
own to say? You are that empty
you turn to bald description? O,
escritor, I feel sorry for you, you who
need to kickstart your own imagination
and even then it only *spu-spu*-sputters.

PARABLES FOR RODIN

1. Portrait of the Sculptor

His beard is an eighteenth-century forest
in south central France.
A wife's thin fingers stroke the tired eyes
of an old man asleep in a hammock.
No sounds issue from his lips.
He is made of bronze.

2. A Letter

Rodin is writing a letter.
Everything points toward this fact—
the sheets of paper, the bowl
of ink, the light from the east
window shining on the pen beside
his hand. The letter is to one
of the illustrious dead.
"Dear Claude Lorrain,"
it begins.

3. The Rodin Tableau

The Hand of the Devil holds
Woman. Fauness kneels. Adonis
lies dead. Headless Woman
bends over. The Secret is
passed between Victor Hugo
and Puvis de Chavannes.
Pulitzer, Clemenceau and
George Bernard Shaw are
called upon to mill. In
the absolute center stands
The Man with the Broken Nose.

4. Guests at the Banquet

Miss Eve Fairfax
Mrs. Potter-Palmer
Madame Eliseieff
Madame Fonaille
Renee Vivien
The Duchesse de Choi Seul
Mrs. Hunter
Maurice Haquette
George Hecq
Pierre de Wiessant
Jean D›aire

5. After the Ball

The Burghers of Calais are hungry.
They are clamoring for food.
"Feed us, feed us!" they cry.
Rodin in full dress
rushes to his studio
to take from the highest shelf
Head of St. John the Baptist
on a Platter.

6. A Vision of Love

A young girl shifts her smooth bronze thigh
and crosses her young bronze leg.
She waits, silent in the studio
amid dust from plaster, blasting,
carving, sanding, and casting.
Enter her lover. With goggles
and blowtorch.

INMATE WORDS

in *White Heat*
there's a character
who reads lips

using a mirror to see
the mouths of prisoners
in other cells

that's how I feel
when I talk
with you

except I don't
need a mirror
to see your lips

except that I don't
know the first thing
about lip reading

except that I'm free
not a prisoner
in a cell

but that's how I feel
when I try to capture
the inmate words

that attempt
their daytime
escape

from the lithe
penitentiary
of your mouth

MANET NIGHTMARE
to Osric

The tall, thin ectomorph sat
on the verdant, green grass

as the unclothed naked woman
on the Sunday-picnic blanket

poured white cow's milk
into a vodka shot glass.

Overhead a two-winged bird,
flying fast, moved quickly across

a stuffed, cotton-puffed,
robin's-egg, light-blue sky

as two swimming swans swam by
pale white in the whispering wave.

MAGRITTE

1. Introduction to Magritte

I pick Magritte up from the bottom of a star.
He is desolate with lavender.
"Who is it?" he moans, touching my wrist
with his wing. I help him to his feet,
careful of his cedar leg.
Behind his grimace he is smiling.
Like a man drowning in warm water.

2. First Experience—Dawn

We climb through a busted window.
Magritte cuts his arm. Blood drops out
like rusty pennies. A mermaid
standing on wet gravel waves to us.
He doffs his bowler.
The black paraffin that fills his head
spills out.
This always happens.

"What's in your palm?" he asks.
She opens it.
It's a baby oyster
covered in cobweb.

3. Second Experience—Midmorning

The day's as gray as a century of salmon eggs.
One sun-pocked building catches my attention.
"No," he says. "Under this arch."
We cobble our way through old streets,
pass vegetable merchants, occasional hunchbacks,
daughters yet to be consecrated.

Arriving at the pier I see a sailboat in dead wind.
"That is pathos," Magritte says,
pointing to a barnacle.

4. *The Woman*

She folds and unfolds her kerchief
folding her eyes in her lap.
Her fingers are long and drawn and thin
like hollow reeds or scabbards.
She is all meekness, all pastel.
We see her at the scaffold
darkening in the air
where the clouds are heaving like minstrels
and the hawks watch as they fly.
Her majesty derives from open clouds
yet she derives from twilight.
We salute her in tandem
and gasp as her voice rises
and rises into our eyes.

5. *Toledo*

That evening, stepping over lengthening shadows,
we are in Toledo where the moon
appears as the white bone of a rose,
where four clouds create the horizon,
where four sounds echo through the trees.
At the curtain of the city
we come across a thin strand of finger
belonging to El Greco.

"Give that to the woman,"
says Magritte.
"She has more need of the digit
than we."

6. *Bedtime Narrative*

And on that day, the Creator said to Speech, "What makes your skin flat like the river? I shall give you wounds to perform in your flesh so that you may never be plain to me." And He was pleased with the lesion which He called Silence and touched His lips to the sky. That place, today, is forbidden to birds.

7. *Waking*

Now the tendon of God is stretched to plain view.
A million onions have been carried to the mirror.
Long birds fly in broken formation.
All is amethyst and milk.
Without warning the white sword
crashes down on orthodoxy.
The sky splits open like Hell's abortion.
A Saracen sun advances on Magritte.

Be Sadistic

FREE BLURBS

1. I read this book religiously and thought "For the love of God!"

2. This book is not easy to forget, but I'm trying.

3. If I had it to do all over again, I don't think I'd even *start* this book.

4. This is a book only a mother could love; sadly for you, I am not a mother.

5. This is the kind of bad book that gives other bad books a bad name.

6. I've read books like this before but never with such remorse.

7. You can't afford not to not read this book.

8. If you're looking for a pleasant way to pass two hours, watch an old movie.

9. If you're addicted to reading, I believe I may be holding your cure.

10. Of the making of bad books there is no end. Don't believe me? See Lulu, but not just Lulu.

PROMPTS

Write a poem beginning with the word "bed"
in which the word "horse" or "alpine"
appears in the seventh line.

Write a poem in which fraternal twins
each marry accountants.

Write a poem in which the last letter of the third word in every line
spells out your home state.

Write a poem in which your father is a dog
and you are his leash.

Write a poem containing seven sixteen-syllable words

Write a poem of 1000 lines
in which prime numbers figure prominently.

Write a poem whose first word is also its last word
whose 2nd word is also its 11th word
whose 43rd word is also its 6th, 17th, and 69th word
and whose 95th word is a foreign word.

Write a poem in which Christian missionaries
become dry cleaners.

Write a poem made entirely
of refrains.

Write a poem in which your best friend
marries your worst enemy.

Write a poem whose syllables
number 613.

Write a poem in which the narrator
is the weather.

Write a poem in which the spirit of your dead cat
tells you what to write your next poem about.

Write a poem that does not contain the word
"poem."

PLANE OF POETS

The plane was filled with poets!
Cold inspiration was in the air!
The green-haired poet!
The doe-eyed poet!
The booted poet! The bootless poet!
The mannequin poet! The poet manqué!
The bejeaned, bejeweled, and begrimed poet!
The baggy-skin poet and the bagatelle poet!
The blistering, blustery, fustian poet!
The hootin' poet! The Putin poet! The root toot tootin' poet!
The budding poet! The balding poet!
The King of Sonnets and his regina, Queen Sestina!
The poet of scarves! The poets in hats! The lone-cufflink poet!
The bottle poet! The blotto poet!
The yeast poet and the dough poet!
The baked poet and the half-baked poet!
The mottled poet in motley cloak!
The contused poet! The bemused poet! The abused poet!
The slob poet! The mob poet! Bob, the poet!
The tattooed, tongue-pierced, ear-gauged poet!
O Poets! Poets! Poets!
Poets so anxious! Poets in a rush!
Go! Go! File past me.
Get thee to thy writing desks!
What wonders you will write!

THE 'MODERN' POETS

I've been reading *The Modern Poets* edited by Brinnin and Read
but it's not the poems but the p·h·o·t·o·g·r·a·p·h·s
that are the most interesting pages: all those
ANTIQUE poets looking so so so **PRISTINE**!

How many hold cigarettes!
      How many in jackets and ties!
            How many turn sideways!
                  How many stare directly at us!

Brinnin posing at Stonehenge with a pipe
  Betjeman dressed in clothes "that once belonged to Henry James."
   Robert Graves in profile in a Spanish hat

  Thom Gunn in leather jacket and studded leather belt
Daniel Hoffman looking impish with I. B. Singer ears
  Anthony Hecht in a work shirt doing his best Richard Conte

    Robert Lowell standing meaningfully against a falling wall
  like he's auditioning for a role in an Antonioni film

The unexpectedly bright-eyed Ted Hughes
  Predictably disheveled Frost
    Wrinkly John Ciardi dressed like the uncle you just lost

I flip between the photographs of Donald Hall and Dylan Thomas
    Their bold cigars and wacky resemblance!

I stare at the picture of Delmore Schwartz
  (his "Baudelaire" the best poem in the volume)
    looking back at the phantom creditors gaining on him

James Scully's portrait forecasts a slovenly 60's insolence.

But against all the foolishness and falsity

    of these poet portraits

there is the Renaissance face
                    of Edith Sitwell
                                        dressed and framed in black
                              whose hooded eyes and oval
                         inwardness are honest
          like all really good poems

POETS WHO THRUM

Poets who thrum like larkspur and bramble and hedgerow
Poets who thrum glaze the drape of their cadmium frame
Poets who thrum like lacewings, sobriquets, and krill
Poets who thrum intercalate interstitial fancy
Poets who thrum go "pukka, pukka, pukka"
Poets who thrum eschew cochineal shoes

Poets who thrum are clart with hebetude
Poets who thrum are thrawn in the gloaming
Poets who thrum groak
Poets who thrum also brabble
Poets who thrum plitter
Poets who thrum also ukase

Poets who thrum jirble and thwack
Poets who thrum eat quorn with raw swamms
Poets who thrum are eristic (not shambolic)
Poets who thrum deliciate unto kench when they freck
Poets who thrum furl their hops and fudgel their tongs
Poets who thrum exsuperate manuka while they mugger and thumb

Some of my best friends are poets who thrum

THE FAMOUS WRITERS I LIKE

The famous writers I like
as human beings
were mostly **monsters**

More than a few
were **totally**
reprehensible

By and large, the famous writers I like
were **not** people
I would have ever liked to meet

Where can you find a **real** asshole?
Check out some of the famous
writers I like

THE INTERVENTION
for Joani Reese

Part One

A horde of well-intentioned poets I had met online
descended upon Lake Forest where I had
gone to attend a lecture entitled "Jung Love."
They accosted me outside the hall and dragged
me to a craft brewery where, in a back room
decorated with stainless knives, they surrounded
me and then drew their circle tighter. "Kid," they
said solemnly, "you're publishing too much too
quickly. We think that's unhealthy. We want you
to slow down. You're becoming a fame whore."

A fame whore!? I shouted. *I have as much integrity
as any poet here!* and then I paused as the absurdity
of my words dripped, like dark irony, down my legs.

I look around the room at the sharp noses and
bulbous heads of the assembled poets come to
save me—from myself—but when had that ever
worked? Hadn't Kleist taught us there's no rescue,
none whatsoever? What were they going to do
anyway—get me banned from Submittable?

I brandished my new manuscript. *You'll never
stop me! Never! Never!* Wriggling free from the grip
of their overdeveloped index fingers, I ran out
into the octave of streets and signs, hissing,
You dare tell me *what not to do? Me!
Hear me, recreants! I'm unfriending
the whole rotten lot of you!*

Part Two

—Have the nightmares subsided any? the lady in white queried.
—Do you mean have they lessened in frequency? Yes. But not in intensity. I still feel pursued by harpies. They tear at the buttons of my Beethoven pajamas! They threaten to boil my brains within my skull! Yesterday, they threatened to laminate my writing hand!
—Now, now. Take it easy. No one's going to do any tearing or boiling or laminating around here. You can rest easy.
—Where's my manuscript? What have you done with my manuscript?
—It's quite safe. We've locked it in the vault as you requested.
—Bring it to me! Bring it to me! I need to see it. There's something I need to fix.
—Why don't you try to get some sleep? You can fix it later.
— [*Shouting*] I don't have time for later! Later is just the foul excrescence of now! [*Screaming*] I'm being tortured by the muddy suddenness of sudden muddiness!!! [*Begins beating at his head, violent thrashing from side to side*]
—Ssshhh. Go to sleep, my little poet. [*Administers sedative*] Go to sleep, you benign trollop.

Part Three

—We'd like to ask you a few questions. Is that OK with you?
—[*Silence*]
—Name?
—Name. Same. Fame. Lame.
—Age?
—How old? All tolled? All bold. Resold.
—Do you know where you are?
—Are? Car. Jar. Far.
—Do you know who I am?
—Am? Yam. I yam what I yam. Popeye the sailor man. Popeye and Olive. Olive Oil. Oil for love. Oil's well that ends oil. Oil you need is love. [*Begins to dance*] Love is oil you need.
—There, there. Sit down. Please? It'll be OK if you just sit down. I promise you it will be OK. You have my word.
—Word bird. Word merde. Word deterred. Word inferred. Word absurd. Word is turd.

HOW POETS DIE

MARK STRAND

over decades
a steady diet of diction
enlarged his heart

one day it just burst

ROBERT FROST

a crazy idea
that he could
build a wall
without mortar took
possession of his mind

he piled stone
on stone higher
and higher until
they toppled over
crushing him beneath

WILFRED OWEN

a bullet (not his own)
to the brain

DYLAN THOMAS

he did not die
from alcohol poisoning
as many believe

rather, early on
his brain caught fire

and it took
twenty-two years
to burn itself out

T.S. ELIOT

hardening of the
sensibility

ALLEN GINSBERG

run over
by New Jersey

WALLACE STEVENS

overdose
of indemnity

WILLIAM CARLOS WILLIAMS

He a (pedia
tri-cian)   died

when
he dis
   covered

his pre-scriptions

      could

             no

                    l o n g e r

        be   ful-fill-ed

John Berryman

jumped off
Hart Crane's
                    bridge

Hart Crane

born
without ears

it was just a matter of time

Be Forensic

8 NEW WAYS OF LOOKING AT WAFFLES

1. the mind (in its righteousness)
waffles

2. the conscience (in its scrupulousness)
waffles

3. the heart (in its cupidity)
waffles

4. the soul (in its annihilation)
waffles

5. the tongue (in its appeasement)
waffles

6. the skin (in its lethargy)
waffles

7. the body (in its luxury)
waffles

8. life (in its delirium)
waffles

THINGS I LEARNED BUT NO LONGER BELIEVE

Shakespeare had red hair
Van Gogh never painted a nude

Apollinaire was a pornographer
Satie wore corduroy suits

Schiller sniffed moldy apples
Edward Lear colored trees

Balzac used a raven's quill
Hamsun survived TB

Sherwood Anderson was a Zionist
Zane Grey was a doc

Radiguet owned land in Lebanon
Mencken lived in hock

Groucho Marx read Eliot's eulogy
Thackeray seduced his maid

Edward Dahlberg's dog was Mala
Rimbaud's buried in Marseilles

Joyce was allergic to chocolate
Melville played the sax

Hart Crane had wet dreams
Chandler spayed his cats

Woolf posed naked for Freud
Goethe was four feet tall

D.H. Lawrence voted for Eisenhower
Borges owned a mall

Chekhov carted oysters
Stendhal sweated art

Poe had a canary named Ligeia
Flaubert stole Baudelaire's heart

THE GRILLED SAINT

I celebrate Saint Lawrence
who was broiled on a gridiron
and whose seaway is impressive.
He is the patron saint of curriers
those who dress, finish and color leather
to make it strong, flexible waterproof, and pretty.
For conspiring to hide Church documents, librarians also claim him.
When asked to turn over the Church's riches
he brought before the Roman prefect the poor, blind, ragged and infirm.
These, he said, *are the true treasures of the Church*
at which point they seized him and placed him atop burning coals.

After some time he is reputed to have remarked,
Turn me over. I'm done on this side.
Thus he is claimed not only by cooks and chefs
but also by comedians.

But was he really that droll as he was being burned alive?

The Reverend Patrick Joseph Healy argues
this was all the result of an innocuous error
the unwitting omission of the letter p
by which the solemn formula
for announcing the death of a martyr
—*passus est*—
was made to read *assus est,*
passus est meaning *he suffered*
assus est meaning *he was roasted*

That's how the disparaging proverb
he's as lazy as Lawrence
got started and spread across the centuries
for that was what his tormentors said about the martyr
as he lay supine on the burning grill
a man apathetic and listless
too indolent, they thought, *even to wriggle.*

- Apperson, George Latimer and Martin Manser. *Dictionary of Proverbs*. Ware, Hertfordshire: Wordsworth Editions Limited, 1993.
- Benet, William Rose. *The Reader's Encyclopedia*, 2nd edition. Thomas Y. Crowell & Co., 1965.
- Healy, Patrick Joseph. *The Valerian Persecution: a Study of the Relations between Church and State in the Third Century*. Boston and New York: Houghton, Mifflin, and Company, 1905.
- Wikipedia, the Free Encyclopedia: https://en.wikipedia.org/wiki/Lawrence_of_Rome. Accessed 24 September, 2015.

THE BALD EAGLE

Prof: Romantic poetry is exclamatory poetry, the poetry of the exclamation mark.
Grad: You mean like in Wordsworth? "I feel! I feel it all!"

Prof: Milton was the first Romantic.
Grad: Are you saying Romantic poetry begins with *Sampson Agonistes*?

Prof: Modernism begins with Cowper. The first authentic anguished 'I' in litera-
ture appears in the last stanza of "The Castaway."
Grad: I think I understand.

Prof: Over time, all human codes get broken. The indecipherable becomes
transparent.
Grad: Like the works of Faulkner, Eliot, and Joyce?

Prof: Meanwhile, time makes mysteries out of clarities. The transparent becomes
indecipherable.
Grad: Like the jokes in Shakespeare, Jonson, and Pope?

Prof: Now, the eighteenth century's dark heart is not, as is commonly thought, de
Sade.
Grad: Perhaps Dr. Johnson? In his prayers and meditations?

Prof: In my opinion, of all the important critics, Coleridge, far and away, caused the
greatest harm.
Grad: Who caused the least?

Prof: The epitome of velocity assuredly is *Candide*.
Grad: Well, the opening chapters for sure.

Prof: Proust is a perfumed sewer.
Grad: Hrrrrrummmph!

Prof: What did you think of Ted Hughes' *Birthday Letters*?
Grad: The poetry, I think, is in the exhumation.

Grad: Delmore Schwartz is the Barbara Payton of American poetry.
Prof: Barbara Payton? Who is Barbara Payton?

Grad: Gogol's *Dead Souls*: an allegory of Facebook. Everyone on Facebook is Chichikov.
Prof: I'm not sure I follow you, my boy.

Grad: In *The Waste Land*, the learning's a joke; only the feeling is real.
Prof: After many years of wasted research, I've come to that conclusion myself.

THE SEPARATION

wrote Yeats:

    The intellect of man

            is forced to choose

                perfection of the art

                    or of the life

      who was Yeats to posit that separation?

                    I pondered Yeats
                  I pondered my heart

                  I pondered my past
               I pondered my children

                  I pondered my marriage.
               I pondered my future

        I concluded

life is rich

    pudding

                    life is rough

             soup

THE MIRROR TIRES OF LOOKING AT ITSELF

We are all essays, some poorly written,
some sparkling prose. The best of us
has a thesis, a goal which organizes
our lives. We prove our claims
as we go. Transitions are our friends.
We move toward conclusion, but others
will have the final word. In heaven, we get
edited. We are read by those we leave behind.

Sure, to a teacher, life is a term paper
but what would life be to a druggist?
Surely he'd have other ideas. What about
a dry cleaner? A barista? The safety inspector?
Resort concierge? Auto mechanic? Hedge-fund
manager? Discrimination attorney? The golf pro?
Have you asked the butcher's daughter?
Have you approached the neighborhood fellatrice?

DARBY TAKES ME TO THE PLAYBOY CLUB TO SEE REDD FOXX

I.

Back in the 70's when there were Playboy Clubs,
I went to one. My feminist girlfriend took me
on her sexist father's membership. Being college
students of the time, we pretended to get dressed up,
and they sat us, reluctantly, at a little table in the back
with one lonely lamp with a lace lampshade on it.
We ordered spicy drinks and a busty woman
my mom's age served us. It was dark and smoky
as Redd Foxx came out to great applause.

Foxx, known for his "blue" nightclub material,
was predictably filthy. I was embarrassed for
my girlfriend who stonily endured the vulgarity
of his act. Well, what did we expect? We were
in a Playboy Club in upper New Jersey
watching a famous dirty comedian perform.

Later that night, in her parents' living room,
Darby came to me after everyone else had gone
to bed. I thought she was coming to say good night
(I was visiting from out of town and sleeping on her
couch), but she wanted to make love.

> "Here? In your living room?"
> *No one will bother us. My mom said it was OK.*

So that night, over our winter break, we made love
on the carpeted floor. She wanted to replace
the memory of the outside world with something
less crass, and, at the time, I was all there was.

II.

Wait a minute—Darby was a feminist and she
agreed to go to a Playboy Club? What kind of
feminist was she? Whose idea was it to go
in the first place? If the performance was
offensive and made Darby uncomfortable,
why didn't you and she get up and leave?
Darby's mother gave Darby permission
to have sex with you on the living room
floor? Did Darby ask her mom? Did the mom
offer first!? The sexist dad was OK with that?
What, was the mother pushing the daughter
on you? To what end? Marriage? Are you kidding
me? What kind of marriage did Darby's parents
have? The father was a male chauvinist with a key
to the local Playboy Club and the mother encouraged
premarital sexual relations with her daughter and a
strange boy? What happened to Darby? Did she break
up with you or did you break up with her? Is this why
you never got married? Is this why you moved away?

PROVERBS OF THE CONVERTED

a journey of a thousand miles begins with a single
ticket

a person is known by the company he
shuns

a good man is hard to
solicit

a house divided against itself cannot
multiply

where there's a will, there is
death

if you lie down with poets, you'll get up with
bullshit

Be Ballistic

WE ALL SAW IT COMING

We all saw it coming
the snakes in ascendance
the dark satanic milling around
the troops of the nouveau greedy
the safety nets on fire
the cesspool of superiority
flooding the brazen stage

We all saw it coming
the peat moss racists
the neonatal Nazis
King Leer
Queen Get-rude
the bully trident planted
the ratcheting down of sense

We all saw it coming
the tide of crude insurgence
complacency swept away
virtue's camel toe exposed
the nipple slip of decency
the fondling of the tit of turpitude
the gangbang of the plebiscite

We all saw it coming
I don't mean we
I don't mean we saw it coming

I mean I, I saw it coming
and did nothing

A BRAVE NIGHT TO COOL A COURTESAN

after *King Lear* III, ii, 81-94

When iodine coffee is promoted by aging surgeons
when arsonists masquerade as first responders
when phantasmagoric nuns mock the lisps of addicts
when Internet juveniles arouse the spleen of gamblers
when the library asylum is redistricted by radio politics
when adjunct bank examiners call on extortionists for help
when the rooftop pool is overrun by media beetles
when evangelical bobcats weaponize the electorate
when legal Satans unhook Christ's suspenders
then shall the whorish country bow down to trumpery

GO, UNLOVELY TRUMP
after Edmund Waller

Go, unlovely Trump—
tell the horse-faced Putin
you will play his rump
and bow to his delirium
with expectations of asylum.

Go, unlovely Trump—
dupe of exploitation,
cesspool, human dump—
bid farewell to the irked nation
for your treasons are unwelcome.

Small is the worth
of bluster from facts retired:
I bid you go forth
and suffer, undesired,
and not blush ever, you, eternally unadmired.

THE HOLLOW PRESIDENT

after T. S. Eliot

You are the hollow man
You are the stuffed man
Pumpkin head filled with straw.
Alas!

   The wind whispers:

      P-u-t-i-n . . .

Eyes I dare not meet in dreams
in death's dream kingdom!
Let me be no nearer!
Not that final meeting
in the twilight kingdom!

   The wind whispers:

      P-u-t-i-n . . .

This is the dead land (no, not yet)
This is cactus land (no, not yet)
Here the stone images are raised
(no, no) here they receive
the approbation of a man's
tiny hand (no, nyet)

   The wind whispers:

      P-u-t-i-n . . .

The eyes are not here
The sense is not here
The heart is not here
Empty man

There are no eyes here
in this valley of dying stars
in this hollow valley
this broken jaw of our lost kingdom

The wind whispers:

P-u-t-i-n . . .
In this last of meeting places
you grope--for what? Not hope.
The wind whispers:

P-u-t-i-n . . .

Here we go round the politics tree
the politics tree, the politics tree
Here we go round the politics tree
at seven fifteen in the morning

Between the idea
and the reality
Between the motion
and the act
fall the People

For Thine is NOT the Kingdom

Between the emotion
and the response
Between the essence
and the descent
fall the People

For Thine is NOT the Kingdom

This is the way the world ends
This is the way the world ends
This is the way the world ends

NO

AMERICA THE MISERABLE
after Katharine Lee Bates

O Misery! For daily lies!
For baleful schemes of gain!
For deportation travesties!
For cruel inflicted pain!
America! America!
Trump's shed disgrace on thee
and crowned thy pate with vicious hate
and stained democracy.

THE APPLICATION OF BIRDS

We read in the *Devotions* of John Donne *Spirante*
columba supposita pedibus, revocantur ad ima vapores
meaning "They apply pigeons to his feet to draw the vapors
from his head," but the word "columba" is ambiguous;
it could also mean "doves." I like the idea of applying
doves to the feet of a sick man better than I like the idea
of applying filthy pigeons to a person's nether extremities
but what does it even mean to "apply" pigeons or doves?
And how does one apply a bird to a man? And how many
birds would it take to draw out those baleful vapors, to effect
a cure? I know someone in need of healing. I know a man
to whom the application of doves could do a positive good,
but he opposes, philosophically, letting doves into his soul.
So I am offering him pigeons, a basket of preening fantails.
Open all your windows! Surround yourself with wings!

THE RINSED MESSIAH

They are come—The Men Who Rue Infinity.

"What is the function of the empty mountain?"
ask The United Dreck of Amalek.

Flâneur! Flâneur!
Flâneurs of rinsed spirit

Paparazzi apparatchiks
from the Kingdom of Dubeity

What percentage of eternity is this our earthly life?

The hard clouds breed insolence
into the fruition
of nutrition.

*Dear Psychomachia,
who is Deep
Threat?*

infected investing
the return of the
oppressed

analysis by paralysis
much doodoo about
everything

*
*
*

*Induce me   Induce me
There's a uterus in your future*

ALL ABOUT THE TUMOR

Stupidity is not a mask; it is the face
and it is the face that betrays us
always. That is the lesson of mirrors.

I was apoplectic about corruption.
I appealed to outside magic, ideas
bright and dark. Sonya solaced me.

Flirting with eternity, strangling
the larynx of the sky, I stood on
edges and matriculated fervency.

I read in the phonemes of the trees
"Happiness is the habit of right reason
practicing vice." My course was set.

I fell in with felons, derogatory
men who lived on the verge of
mercy. They sequenced my DNA

for it was all about the tumor, you see.
For the health of the state, it had to be
ripped away. We used mindfulness.

I recuperated in Sonya's arms. Some days
we think back and remember Abelard:
"It's a wonderful life—until it's not."

Be Acoustic

EL DESDICHADO BY NERVAL
an incompetent translation

I am twilight's pissoir, the orphan's
inclination. My star is dead; my constellation
crushed. The Prince of Aquitaine has fallen
and cannot rise. I am the shadow of waxwing slain.

In the tomb, in the outré tombe, I see
the Sea of Capri, the Hearse of Merci,
La Lune de Pantoum, La Place du Caprice.
Désolé! Désolé! Où le vinaigre et le vin sont un.

I am naked and red, cheri. Give me back
my color and my clothes. Give me back my
singularity, my tristesse, my photo ID.

She sits in a gondola and burnishes her arms.
She puts the piquant radish in her mouth.
She takes a loofa and wipes the rainbow from her neck.

SONG OF UNSELF
after Walt Whitman

I cerebrate myself and singe myself
and what you illume, I refuse
for every good Adam betrothed to you will to me betray

I chafe and incite my soul
I bake and chafe in my disease
my speech, every item of tongue foams in this soil-
free dust

earth's parents ... whose parents ...
arrrrggghhh ... I now sixty-seven
sixty-eight, sixty-nine years

chagrin besmears me, increases
till death, old shoals in obeisance

nothing suffices as harbor
but a permit to claw at every yawing chasm
exuberance is beauty ... lesion of enthusiasm

THE TWO LERMONTOVS

I am in a strip club thinking about
Lermontov, but which? Boris Lermontov,
the Diaghilev of <u>The Red Shoes</u>?

Or Mikhail Lermontov, novelist poet
of "Alone Went Out I on Slender Road"?

I was twenty when I first read his book
and he was twenty-five when he wrote it.

I'm more nihilist now than I was then:
portrait of Pechorin as an old man.

What year was it when the Powell film came on
TV? Blitzkrieg of color and motion!

I wanted all his clothes, his shoes, his shades,
his stance, his walk, his *pas de deux* with art.

Boris Lermontov. Funny name. Funny,
my father's name was Boris. He kept that

to himself. I'm thinking about him now
while watching Sin's twin tits. Something wrong here!

Boris...Mikhail...Boris...Mikhail... Boris

sipping a Gin Rickey on Spring Garden
Street in the shade of Fairmont Park with a

blonde woman (*I see them*) whose granddaughter
(*I imagine*) I am watching beneath

colored flood lights, white seashells on black walls,
whose dewy breasts, eyeing each other like

foes, shake out of synch like a putative
suicide in an antique novel or

postwar film. What is art? asked lithe Tolstoy
and the answer flutters back: "What you suck."

THE DRUNKEN BOAT BY RIMBAUD
an incompetent translation

At five o'clock in the afternoon, at five o'clock
in the afternoon, I got on (or boarded) to embark
the intoxicated dingy, the restive inebriated skiff

of last week's dreams, with a muskrat, cockroach,
and Richard Parker (the CGI tiger from *Life of Pi*)
to drift, elementally and continentally, infinitely

and augustly, past honeymoons and industrial
cantilevers, vats of lovers' hats and laundry,
through boulevards of bacon bits and coarse catacombs

of honey. Who would have thought? I ask you: would you
have thought? And what the sky. And what the pock-marked,
red-faced, foul-mouthed, slim-hipped sky. What price

allegiance? (Circular gunfire in Orion's head) What man has
planted can break his self-regard. Perfume from an unseen
censer. O Jamesy, Jamesy, let me up. Let me up out of this.

SPLEEN BY BAUDELAIRE

an incompetent translation

I am the King of Pleurisy,
rich, importunate, and *very* old.
I despise my raven instructor
tepid as a dog in the mouth of a bell
as pale as the wail of a falcon on a gibbet
as pimpled as a toad on a black *balcón*.
The clown is distraught, his body cruel.
Literature shall transform this tomb
of a whore into a fleur-de-lis.
The poor prince does not yet know
how to improve his base *toilette*
or relieve the *tsouris* of the baby squirrel.
Who can extirpate the corrupt savant
or bathe Vienna in what must be Rome?
Old joys are impotent souvenirs
chauffeured grievously by forgetfulness.

I CHANNEL QUEVEDO

for Age

- Hey, life! Nobody answers? WTF?
- Ah life! Nobody answers me. Well, what did I expect?

- All the years that I have lived, fate, fate has chewed my days.
- Back through the decades I have lived, my days all ripped by fortune.

- My insanity has covered my hours.
- Madness has hidden my time.

- Without knowing how or where, my youth and health have vanished.
- Without the ability to know where or how, my strength and happiness have fled.

- Visiting the living, there's no misery that doesn't surround me.
- Attending to calamity, there's no obligation that doesn't bury me alive.

- Yesterday's gone, tomorrow hasn't arrived, and today is fading.
- Yesterday's dissolved, tomorrow has not yet come, and today without even a "Screw you, buddy" is disappearing on me.

- For much of my life, I have been tired, I may well be tired tomorrow, but today, today I am completely without energy.
- I was, I am, and I will (tired though I am) continue to pretend to exist.

- Yesterday and tomorrow and today, we are all in this dreck together.
- In the today, the tomorrow, and the yesterday, there is no "you," there is no "I," there is just "we."

- Soiled diaper to immaculate shroud, I've witnessed a fucking unending parade of decay!
- Matricides, fratricides homicides, suicides—I've endured a continuous shitload of grief!

"Meaphysical Poem #2" by Francisco Gómez de Quevedo y Santibáñez Villegas

THE TOMB OF BAUDELAIRE BY MALLARMÉ

an incompetent translation

Listen, Svengali, all the museums
are on fire and the Abbé Farouche
has asked me to tell you this: who
polishes the aberrant enshrines it.

So here's the plan: write an essay
on masculinity. Make it puerile and
opprobrious, but do not let it reverberate.
Fashion it of the loosest most recent mesh.

How sketchy are cities without futility!
The votive truth may resonate but what
about the vain marble of salty Beau d'Lair?

O, Popery! El Hombre has left us deficient
as a frozen shadow, as the staunch tutor who,
poisoned, resuscitates but refuses to revive.

THE POEMS OF MARINA ODOROVNA SMULINSKY
[МАРИНА ОДОРОВНА СМУЛИНСКИЙ]

When I was in St. Petersburg in August 1998, I met the owner of an outdoor cafe and we became friends. She and I corresponded over the next two years. Then we fell out of touch. In October 2009, I received a package from her. In it was a manuscript of poems in Russian by Marina Smulinsky, a poet I had never heard of. Also in the package was a letter in English from my friend explaining that Marina was her aunt who had died the previous spring. She explained that her aunt had been "a secret poet," writing but never publishing any of her many poems.

She wondered if I would consider translating them (I had learned Russian in graduate school) and sending them out to magazines to see if there was any interest in publishing them. I wrote her that my Russian was poor and that I was not really a translator. I recommended some other writers I knew better suited for that job. She insisted that only I do the work. She offered to pay me out of the money she inherited after her aunt's death. Reluctantly, I agreed.

It has taken me almost ten years (and many dictionaries) to complete this project. In that time, my friend died from hepatitis. I was never paid the money she promised me, but the money was never that important to me. Much more important are these poems—quite extraordinary in their delicate sensibility and large, inordinate word choice if I understand them at all correctly. These poems are monsters of quiet genius, skirmishes with crazy needlepoint mastery, towering rayon sculptures of fragile ferocity.

It is with humility laced with keen pleasure that I present my inadequate forays into the quixotic alchemy that is translation from the *russkiy yazyk* [Russian language] into *priyemlemyy angliyskiy* [acceptable English].

THE FIRST TEN POEMS

POEM I

o i do not o i do not
right justify j u s t i f i c a t i o n
the pillow's eyesore careSS
Pushkinka! Pushkinka!
why have you foretaken me?
A   A
 T   T
  A   A
   L   L
    A   A
     N   N
      T T
     A

        sigh [[[[[[[

POEM II

that brackishness will not intrude
improve impede impasse that
brackishness will not impress
redo redress exclude improv
outsize incise forswear TEARS
(Come to me. Come to me, Nuna.)
The forest shivers in silver splints.

        sigh [[[[[[[

POEM III

Khrushchev. Gumilev. Doom.
Doom. Doom. Whose lavender
lips do wash me down. Whose
crinoline bodice upstarts my
hear t. The sea is a broken purse.
The future is a wandering net.

        sigh [[[[[[[

POEM IV

Whispers! (*shhhhhsh*) Whispers!
(*shhhusssh*) The sunset is (*shhsh*)
edible. The coffins (*shhssssh!*)
have ears. Lula x Lula = Lula.
Everything endless has its *.

sigh [[[[[[[

POEM V

RaDIOlactate. That is the
crow. Amniocentrifuge.
That is the leaf blower.
Bilatterly. That is the vine.
Speak, Vlademure! Speak!
Utter! EXPRESS!!! On second
mind, o dew rock, *ferme la buisson.*

sigh [[[[[[[

POEM VI

*Train*ing books by Khleb-
nikov are wetbread com-
pared to the rich bread-
sticks of Khodasevich!

sigh [[[[[[[

[books = kh-nee-gee]
[bread = khleb]
[poems = stick-hee]

POEM VII

I have left the cleft in my heart
bereft. I have spoken no token
of love unbroken. I have borrowed
no sorrow foraged tomorrow. I have

grieved no need, deceived no seed.
I have dressed for the fest where I
tested the jest. I have danced in
lined pants with my latest fiance. I
besought, wrought, and taught
what I thought. *But fierce? Were you
fierce?* O yes! I fought. But all came
to naught and aught I knew to rue.

sigh [[[[[[[

POEM VIII

Fire! Ire! The ice of desire!
Dissolved and diminished,
a funeral pyre. Redacted
and acted by those who
conspire. Reviled and
revealed as incontinent
liars. On the shores of
Bakul, there I'll retire.

sigh [[[[[[[

POEM IX

Di di di di di di di
Contumacious suitor

Fi fi fi fi fi fi fi
Extumaceous partner

Yi yi yi yi yi yi yi
Nonagenarian corsair or copse

sigh [[[[[[[

POEM X

Your eyes, Mikhail are tired.
How rounded and diamond they are—like ice water.
How many summers did we rush
like heretics into autodidactic heresy?
How many summers did we crush
the moonlight into galvanized romantic protons?

Shall we, my friend, once again uncover the blue berries?
Shall we go ride (at a gallop) the horse radishes?

Ah, but the years!
The years have made us brittle.
The years have made us burst like sobs
from the throats of tortured larks.

But nothing has changed!
No! It will will will not change!

You, my granite, are loadstone still.
Once I had the mettle to be your metal.
Now I am a locked tin of iron filings.
The past (alas! alas! alas!) is made of
———————————————paper.

      sigh [[[[[[[

Be Linguistic

ETHAN FROME POEM

he seemed a part
of the mute melancholy landscape—
an incarnation of its frozen woe

with all that was warm and sentient
in him fast bound below the surface—
but there was nothing unfriendly in his silence

I simply felt that he lived
in a depth of moral isolation
too remote for casual access

and I had the sense
that his loneliness
was not merely

the result
of his personal plight
tragic as I guessed that to be

but had in it
the profound accumulated cold
of many stark winters

Found poem. From the preface to *Ethan Frome* by Edith Wharton. One phrase deleted, one word modified.

SILAS MARNER POEM

to men of hard toil
        to men of primitive wants
                to men who have been pressed close
                        to men who have never been illuminated
                                to men who present a range of possibilities
                                      to men of enthusiastic religious faith
                              to men whose imagination is almost barren
                    to men of gladness and enjoyment
              to men of pain and mishap
        to men of images
to far wider men
           to men who have fed desire and men who have fed hope
              to men overgrown by recollections
                    to men who are a perpetual pasture to fear

                                            your eyes
                                    your eyes|||your eyes
                            your eyes|||||||||||your eyes
                    your eyes||||||||||||||||||||||||||your eyes
                        your eyes||||||||||||your eyes
                                your eyes|||your eyes
                                      your eyes

                are pretty much like an insect's

              you
                    can't
                          see
                                  much
                        at
                a
                                                time

Found poem. From chapter vii and chapter I of *Silas Marner* by George Eliot.

WILLIAM ADDIS: INDENTURED GENIUS

William Addis of England
is believed to have produced
the first mass-produced
toothbrush in 1780.

In 1770, he was jailed
for causing a riot.

While in prison he decided
that using a rag with soot and
salt on the teeth was ineffective
and could be improved.

One evening, he saved a
small bone from a meal.

He drilled small holes into the bone
and tied tufts of bristles
obtained from one of the guards
into the holes in the bone.

Then he sealed the holes
with glue.

After his release
he started a business
manufacturing toothbrushes
which made him verifiably wealthy.

A largely found poem. Wikipedia. https://en.wikipedia.org/wiki/Toothbrush . Accessed July 17, 2017.

STIMULATED BY MIRACLES

He does great evil who writes false;
therefore should everyone make that straight
which he before bent crooked.

—Ælfric of Eynsham

I.

The Almighty Creator created Angels by *His* divine power
and in His great righteousness gave them their own choice
that they might continue in eternal happiness through obedience

and might also lose that happiness
not through destiny
but for disobedience

His great righteousness would not compel them to either
but gave them their own choice for that is righteousness
that to everyone be allowed his own choice

II.

Now many a man will think and inquire whence the Devil came?
Be it, therefore known to him that
God created as a great Angel him who is now the Devil

but God did not create him as the Devil
but when he was wholly fordone
and guilty towards God

through his great haughtiness and enmity
then became he changed to the Devil
who before was created a great Angel

III.

It is read in historic narratives that John the Evangelist would
marry
and Christ was invited to his nuptials
Then it befell that at the nuptials wine was wanting

Jesus then bade the serving men fill six stone vessels with pure water
and he with his blessing turned the water to noble wine
This is the first miracle that *He* openly wrought in *His* state of man

Now John was so stimulated by that miracle
that he forthwith left his bride in maidenhood
and ever afterwards followed the Lord

IV.

It is probable that some of you know not what circumcision is:
God commanded Abraham that he and his offspring
should hold His covenant that there might be some sign on their bodies

to show that they believed in God
and commanded him to take a sharp-edged flint
and cut off a part of the foreskin

and that token was then as great among believing men
as is now the holy baptism
excepting Christ turn it to a spiritual sense

V.

They were not ripened for slaughter yet they blessedly died
Snatched from their mothers' breasts, they were instantly
committed to the bosoms of Angels

The wicked persecutor could not by any service
so greatly favor those little ones so greatly
as he favored them by the fierce hate of persecution

They are called blossoms of martyrs because they were
as blossoms springing up in the midst of the chill of infidelity
consumed as it were by the frost of persecution

Found poem. From *The Homilies of the Anglo-Saxon Church*, by Ælfric, translated by Benjamin
Thorpe, 1844.

THE RIVER OF THE PARCHED SPIRIT

patriotism
said Johnson
is the last refuge
of a scoundrel

    folly
    said Blake
    is the cloak
    of knavery

        religion
        said Marx
        is the sigh
        of the oppressed

            anxiety
            said Kierkegaard
            is the dizziness
            of freedom

                music
                said Shaw
                is the brandy
                of the damned

                    the river
                    of the parched spirit
                    waters the desert
                    of the thirsty word

JUGGLING

It is a matter of felicitous _____.
I met Robert Frost's daughter at a _____ the other evening.
Life is meagre with me; I am unsatisfied and left always begging for _____.
Anything for some _____now.

I met Robert Frost's daughter at a _____the other evening.
I like _____in a certain way.
Anything for some _____now.
In my own work I find the problem of _____ and _____ becoming
    more and more difficult.

I like _____in a certain way.
I too have a _____ in the last century.
In my own work I find the problem of _____ and _____ becoming
    more and more difficult.
I admit to a slight leaning toward the _____.

I too have a _____ in the last century
Life is meagre with me; I am unsatisfied and left always begging for _____.
I admit to a slight leaning toward the _____.
    It is a matter of felicitous _____.

A pantoum made entirely from redacted lines from *The Letters of Hart Crane 1916-1932*, edited
by Brom Weber, University of California Press, Berkeley and Los Angeles, 1965. Out of copyright.
Internet Archive.

AUTOBIOGRAPHY IN ITALIAN

A 19 anni, ero seduto nei Giardini Boboli leggendo Mickey Spillane.
(At 19, I was sitting in the Boboli Gardens reading Mickey Spillane.)

Al 29, mi hanno mandato al Festival di poesia a Genova.
(At 29, they sent me to the Poetry Festival in Genoa.)

A 39 anni, frequentavo la padrona di Leopardi, travestita dalla saggezza.
(At 39, I was attending to Leopardi's mistress, ill-dressed in wistfulness.)

A 49 anni, il mio unico compagno era Ingrid Bergman nelle sue vesti Rossellini.
(At 49, my only companion was Ingrid Bergman in her Rossellini robes.)

A 59 anni, sotto i cieli di Dante, sopporto placida inferno del decadimento del corpo.
(At 59, under Dantean skies, I endure the placid Hell of the body's decay.)

LIKING IN *THE SCARLET LETTER*

like a flame that sinks down among the late decaying embers
like a floating sea-bird on the long heaves and swells of sound
like the phantasmagoric play of the northern lights

like an uprooted weed that lies wilting in the sun
like a black shadow emerging into sunshine
like ether out of a phial

like a tuft of green moss on a crumbling wall
like a rough blow upon an ulcerated wound
like the stroke of sudden death

like the dome of an immense lamp
like blades of grass at the sweep of the scythe
like a line of cliffs against a tempestuous tide

like a shapeless piece of driftwood tossed ashore
    with the initials of a name upon it
like the voice of a young child that was spending its infancy
    without playfulness
like a ghost that revisits the familiar fireside and can no longer
  make itself seen or felt

like a man taken by surprise in a mood to which he was reluctant
    to have witnesses
like a glimmering light that comes we know not whence
    and goes we know not whither
like the first encounter in the world beyond the grave of two spirits
    who had been intimately connected in their former life but now stood
    coldly shuddering in mutual dread as not yet familiar with their state nor
    wonted to the companionship of disembodied beings

like the convulsive throes of the cholera
like the frozen calmness of a dead woman's features
like one awakening, all nerveless, from an ugly dream

like a young deer
like fading sunshine
like a red flame in the dark

like truth
like a dream
like human language

This poem is composed of similes found in *The Scarlet Letter* (1850) by Nathaniel Hawthorne.

Warning!

If you are easily offended, do NOT read the following essay.

AGAINST PROMPTS

I **never** work from prompts. Here's why.

Prompts are the whips of **someone else's** imagination.

If I say, write a poem in which every other word or every third word or every tenth word tells a different story from the poem as written, I've already done the work for you. Your work is merely filling in the blanks, working it out. You are not the architect. You haven't imagined anything. You haven't envisioned anything. You haven't even thought of anything. Because you are merely a craftsman following a blueprint, neither have you really created anything.

If you take someone else's poem and write your "own" version of that poem (the "After Yeats," "After Stevens," "After Pound," "After Ginsberg," "After Bukowski" model), you haven't really written a poem either. You've just stolen some bones. You've just glued some flesh onto someone else's skeleton.

If I give you a series of five words to use in a poem (let's say: clusterfuck, lily, diamond, ethanol, and twaddle) and you use those five words in your poem, what have you really accomplished? Nothing. Those five words, those denotations, those connotations, those sounds, that mixture—that's mine, not yours.[1] Why do you need me or anyone for a list of words? Why not just look in a dictionary and pick out five words randomly? And if you don't like those five words, pick a different five. Or if you don't like one or two of those five, pick a different one or two. Or pick only four words. Or two words. Or one word.

1
TWADDLE
for Robert P. Kaye (who challenged me to respond to my own prompt)

Lily, you clusterfuck,
if you won't live with me
on my daddy's farm
and grow corn (for
ethanol!) I want my
mama's diamond back.

You like to write from pictures and photos? You need someone else to give you a picture to write about? You need someone else to give you a photo to write about? Go find your own pictures and photos!

You need someone else to tell you to write from a newspaper story? Really?

You need someone else to tell you to look in Homer or Dante or the Bible? Really?

Why do you need someone **outside yourself** telling you what to write about? Have you no inner resources? Have you no self respect?

Are you really so infirm of mind, so deficient in imagination, that you need direction in your writing from other people?[2]

A real poet designs and builds a livable space and makes it elegant and beautiful.

A real poet is an architect who builds, board by board, brick by brick, what he or she imagines.

Are you a real poet or just a house painter?
Are you a real poet or just a tuckpointer?
Are you a real poet or just a squatter?

2

I don't address these questions to students who have no choice but to respond to idiotic prompts of lazy teachers. I have only respect for students who do the best they can with the absurdly silly or intellectually demeaning assignments they are given. I hope though, after they pass their classes, they will, as Christian does in *Pilgrim's Progress*, reach inside themselves for the key which will unlock their own creativity and not rely on outside goads.

This manifesto addresses creative-writing teachers and especially professional creative writers, those writers who write seriously and publish their work. Their reliance on others to tell them what to write about offends me. At its best, a prompt is analogous to playing scales on the piano—a method possibly to develop facility, necessary perhaps for honing a skill, maybe a way to warm up one's hands, but no one in his or her right mind would pay to see a pianist play scales. Thus, let's not pretend any significant work ever came from a prompt. And let's not pretend any serious writer of the past ever worked from prompts.

As I write these words, I am well aware that writers in previous centuries wrote on certain subjects at the behest of patrons, as a result of challenges, and on the occasion or anniversary of certain events. Those may be provocations to creative invention, but they are not prompts in the modern sense of the term. Today, prompts rush in to fill the vacuum of a tired writer's lack of imagination or paucity of ideas. Today, soi-disant writers on social media post things like "I don't know what to write about. Could someone please give me a prompt?" I'm saddened by the wretchedness of such pleas.

In chess, when one does not know which piece to move, one "pushes" a pawn, a poor strategy. In a writing workshop or creative-writing class, when one is at a loss to know what to say or do, one too often "gives" a prompt, not the best use of time. I'd like to see the heavy reliance on prompts to fill time in a workshop or structure a writing class disappear. No legitimate workshop leader or competent teacher ever needs to tell students what to write about, that is to say, to dictate (or even influence) subject matter. Empower students to write; don't insult them by fettering their imaginations.

Against Prompts

Some sample poetry prompts from *Poets & Writers:*

1. **Desert Island**: "If you found yourself stranded on a desert island, what would you most want to have with you? Make a list of ten things—...and then write a poem with the items in your order of importance. Include the reasons why you can't live without each item. Are there specific memories attached to certain items that persuaded you to choose them?" [Pardon me while I vomit.]

2. **Dog Days**: "...Explore other natural occurrences that coincide with summer—...fire rainbows, foxfire, midnight sun—and write a poem in tribute to the hottest days of the year." [Jesus, save me from such a poem!]

3. **A New Direction**: "... This week, choose a short poem—and cross out the last line. Read it again now without its last line, and imagine how the poem might take a different turn at this juncture. Write a continuation of the poem, allowing it to travel to an entirely new conclusion." [Hey, why not try "The Emperor of Ice Cream" by Wallace Stevens? If that works well, then try your hand at "The Second Coming" by William Butler Yeats!]

A quick search on the Internet reveals hundreds (conservative estimate) of people and sites offering writing prompts, and thousands (more likely tens of thousands) of mind-numbing prompts, but it's too easy and too cruel to mock them with quotation, so I'll refrain.

Hey, why not write a poem with the word "refrain" meaning "to stop oneself from doing something" as a refrain in that very poem! Then **refrain** from trying to get that poem published—it's not your idea anyway!

Aphorisms on prompts:

*   Writing from a prompt is nothing more than connecting the dots.

*   Working from a prompt is like cooking from a cookbook: no art there.

*   Nothing original ever came out of someone telling you what to do.

*   The only thing a prompt ever produced is production.

*   Prompts are the cancer of creativity: they metastasize shit.

*   If you need a prompt to write, you may as well just give up.

ACKNOWLEDGMENTS

- "8 New Ways of Looking at a Waffle" was published in *Gloom Cupboard* and appears in *The Lice of Christ*
- "A Brave Night to Cool a Courtesan" appears in *We All Saw It Coming* as "I'll Speak a Prophecy, Then I'll Go"
- "A Thousand Books" was published in *Thunderclap!*
- "Against Prompts" is housed at academia.edu
- "All About the Tumor" was published in *Third Wednesday*
- "Arcade" was published in *Mojave River Review*
- "Auden at Swarthmore" was published in *Olentangy Review*
- "Autobiography in Italian" was published in *Atomic Theory Micro Press*
- "Dali's Temptation of Saint Anthony" was published in *Up the Staircase* and appears in *The Lice of Christ*
- "El Desdichado by Nerval" was published in *treehouse* and appears in *Incompetent Translations and Inept Haiku* as "Incompetent Translation: El Desdichado"
- "End Game" was published in *Moss Trill*
- "Ethan Frome Poem" was published in *Unlost*
- "Get a Grip" was published in *Right Hand Pointing*
- "Go, Unlovely Trump" appears in *We All Saw It Coming*
- "How Poets Die" was published in *Atomic Theory Micro Press*
- "I Channel Quevedo" was published in *Into the Void*
- "Inmate Words" was published in *Olentangy Review*
- "John of God, Painted by Murillo" was published in *Blue Fifth Review* and appears in *The Lice of Christ*
- "Juggling" was published in *Otoliths*
- "Kneecapping the Muse" was published in *Thrice Fiction*
- "Liking in *The Scarlet Letter*" was published in *Olentangy Review*
- "Magritte" was published in *Central Park: A Journal of the Arts and Social Theory*, republished in *Skidrow Penthouse* and appears in *Pointed Sentences*
- "Manet Nightmare" was published in *Festival Writer*
- "Par Delicatesse" was published in *Counterexample Poetics* and appears in *Incompetent Translations and Inept Haiku*
- "Parables for Rodin" was published in *Rio Grande Review*
- "Plane of Poets" was published in *Olentangy Review*
- "Playing Boggle with Lowell's Mind" was published in *Right Hand Pointing*
- "Poets Who Thrum" was published in *Ygdrasil*
- "Prompts" was published in *Caravel Literary Arts Journal*
- "Proverbs of the Converted" was published in *Ygdrasil*
- "Self Inventory" was published in *Pirene's Fountain*
- "Song of Unself" was published in *treehouse* and appears in *Incompetent Translations and Inept Haiku*

- "Speaking to the Dead" was published in *(b)OINK*
- "Spleen by Baudelaire" was published in *OF ZOOS*
- "Stimulated by Miracles" was published in *Humanities Opposition World League* and appears in *We All Saw It Coming*
- "The Application of Birds" was published in *Humanities Opposition World League* and appears in *We All Saw It Coming*
- "The Bald Eagle" was published in *Alephi*
- "The Body in the Other Room" was published in *Ragazine*
- "The Drunken Boat by Rimbaud" was published in *treehouse* and appears in *Incompetent Translations and Inept Haiku* as "Incompetent Translation: Le Bateau ivre"
- "The Famous Writers I Like" was published in *Otoliths*
- "The Grilled Saint" was published in *Humanities Opposition World League*
- "The Hollow President" was published in *Home Planet News Online*
- "The Intervention" was published in *Ginosko Literary Journal*
- "The Mirror Tires of Looking at Itself" was published in *The Brown Boat*
- "The 'Modern' Poets" was published in *The Miscreant*
- "The River of the Parched Spirit" was published in *Blue Fifth Review*
- "The Rinsed Messiah" was published in *Unlikely Stories*
- "The Separation" was published in *Otoliths* and appears in *The Lice of Christ*
- "The Tomb of Baudelaire by Mallarme" was published in *Unlikely Stories*
- "The Two Lermontovs" appears in *Incompetent Translations and Inept Haiku*
- "Things I Learned but No Longer Believe" was published in *Literary Orphans*
- "Tripe and Cocaine" was published in *FIVE:2:ONE*
- "Unseenly" was published in *One Sentence Poems*
- "Ways of Seeing: Carracci" was published in *Fulcrum* and appears in *We All Saw It Coming*
- "We All Saw It Coming" appears in *We All Saw It Coming*
- "Whoami" was published in *Eastern Iowa Review*
- "William Addis: Indentured Genius" was published in *Home Planet News Online*

Thank you to the editors and the publishers of the journals in which these poems, sometimes in slightly altered form, appeared.

Thank you to the members of the Poets Club of Chicago who workshopped a number of these poems.

Thank you to Pam Miller, Nina Corwin, and Susan Slaviero who, as members of the There's No Crying in Poetry writing group, also workshopped a number of these poems.

Thank you, Jane Carman, not just for your belief in and support of this book, but also for your talent, your professionalism, and your friendship. You are always fair, always kind, and generous beyond measure.

Bill Yarrow, Professor of English at Joliet Junior College and an editor at the online journal *Blue Fifth Review*, is the author of *The Vig of Love*, *Blasphemer*, *Pointed Sentences*, and five chapbooks. His work also appears in many national and international journals and in the anthologies *Aeolian Harp, Volume One; This is Poetry: Volume II: The Midwest Poets;* and *Beginnings: How 14 Poets Got Their Start*. He has been nominated eight times for a Pushcart Prize.